VAT RE

HANDBOO.. (UK)

How to Prepare, Reconcile and File a VAT Return to HMRC

STERLING LIBS FCCA

VAT RETURN HANDBOOK

Copyright © 2020 by Sterling Libs

www.sterlinglibs.com

STER ING
LI B S

London, United Kingdom

ISBN Number: 9798668164622

PREFACE – NOTE TO THE READER

You usually submit a VAT Return to HM Revenue and Customs (HMRC) every 3 months. This period of time is known as your 'accounting period.'

There are a number of VAT schemes in use and the one being illustrated in this book is the standard accounting scheme. You can find out more about VAT and specifically about VAT schemes by visiting HMRC website at *https://www.gov.uk/search?q=vat+schemes*

I have been training and mentoring a number of accounting trainees and graduates on various aspects of practical accounting, and VAT is one of those areas of tax compliance that at first seems so complicated and difficult but after doing a couple of them, you will realise that it is not that complicated after all.

So, I hope you will find this to be true for you as have indeed many of my trainees. The illustrations and steps I describe in this book are really very simple to follow.

Check it out.

Sterling Libs FCCA, London UK

DISCLAIMER

This book is designed to provide information on practical work experience on how to prepare, reconcile and submit a VAT return in HMRC free software, Sage 50 accounts and QuickBooks online accounting software. It is sold with the understanding that the publisher and author are not engaged in rendering legal, accounting or other professional services. If legal or other expert assistance is required, the services of a competent professional should be sought.

It is not the purpose of this handbook/reference guide to reprint all information that is otherwise available to accounting students, trainees, graduates or any other accounting professionals, but instead to complement, amplify and supplement other texts. You are urged to read all available material, learn and practice as much as possible about practical accounting and how to do related accounting roles in business and tailor the information to your individual needs.

Every effort has been made to make this book as complete and accurate as possible. However, there may be mistakes, both typographical and in content. Therefore, this text should be used only as a general guide and not as the ultimate source of preparing VAT Returns (UK). Furthermore, this book contains information on day to day regular tasks on how to prepare, reconcile and submit VAT Return (UK) using Sage 50 Accounts and QuickBooks online software current only up to the printing date.

TABLE OF CONTENTS

ABOUT THE AUTHOR

Sterling Libs FCCA, is a fellow of the Association of Chartered Certified Accountants and the author of several books on practical accounting and on how to succeed as an accounting professional.

He runs his own accounting firm in Canary Wharf London.

Sterling is so passionate about helping young aspiring accounting professionals to better understand how accounting is done in practice.

He has championed UK practical work experience in accountancy training which has helped many individuals - (ACCA students & Affiliates, AAT students, CIMA students/Affiliates, university students and graduates in accounting and also those who are already working but want more in-depth practical experience in accounting), and as a direct result many of them have got accounting jobs in the UK.

Sterling is really gifted in making the seemingly complex simple and throughout his books he shows you fundamental and detailed illustrations with examples of how he does that.

Be successful in all you do and remember that Success is a progressive realization of a worthy ideal.

ABOUT VAT

What is VAT?

VAT is a tax on consumer spending. It is added to the cost of most goods and services supplied in the UK and Isle of Man by VAT-registered businesses and paid by the customer. VAT registered businesses can recover some of the VAT they pay on purchases and expenses.

If your business is not VAT registered but you wish to register it, you can do it online, and this includes partnerships, and also group of companies (which can actually register under one VAT number). By registering online, you will create a VAT online account (sometimes known as a 'Government Gateway account'). You need this to submit your VAT Returns to HM Revenue and Customs (HMRC).

Alternatively, you can also appoint an accountant (or agent) to help you register for VAT and submit your VAT Returns and deal with HMRC on your behalf.

You **cannot** register online if:
- you want to apply for a 'registration exception'
- you are joining the Agricultural Flat Rate Scheme
- you are registering the divisions or business units of a body corporate under separate VAT numbers

In those circumstances, you must register by post using **VAT1 form** instead.

Register by post using form:

- VAT1A if you're an EU business 'distance selling' to the UK
- VAT1B if you import ('acquire') goods worth more than £85,000 from another EU country
- VAT1C if you are disposing of assets on which 8th or 13th Directive refunds have been claimed

When you receive your VAT number from HMRC, you can sign up for a VAT online account (select option 'Submit VAT returns').

When to register for VAT

1. You must register for VAT if your VAT taxable turnover goes over £85,000 (the 'threshold'), or you know that it will. Your VAT taxable turnover is the total of everything sold that is not VAT exempt.

How to calculate the taxable turnover and what to include

To check if you've gone over the threshold (£85,000) in any 12-month period, add together the total value of your UK sales that are not VAT exempt, including:

- goods you hired or loaned to customers
- business goods used for personal reasons
- goods you bartered, part-exchanged or gave as gifts
- services you received from businesses in other countries that you had to 'reverse charge'
- building work over £100,000 your business did for itself

Include any zero-rated items - only exclude VAT-exempt sales, and goods or services you supply outside of the UK.

If you are over the threshold, you must register for VAT - though HMRC may allow you 'exception from registration' if your turnover goes above the threshold temporarily.

2. You must register straight away if you expect the value of everything you sell in the next 30 days to be over £85,000. It is compulsory. You do not need to include anything that is VAT exempt.

You have to register by the end of that 30-day period. Your effective date of registration is the date you realised, not the date your turnover went over the threshold.

Example On 1 June, you realise that your VAT taxable turnover in the next 30-day period will take you over the threshold. You must register by 30 June. Your effective date of registration is 1 June.

You must also register if, by the end of any month, your total VAT taxable turnover for the last 12 months was over £85,000.

You have to register within 30 days of the end of the month when you went over the threshold. Your effective date of registration is the first day of the second month after you go over the threshold.

Example: Between 10 August 20XX and 9 August 20X1 your VAT taxable turnover was £100,000. That's the first time it has gone over the VAT threshold. You must register by 30 September 20X1. Your effective date of registration is 1 October 20X1.

You should check your rolling turnover regularly if you're close to going over the threshold.

Note: You can also check historical information about VAT thresholds if you think you should have been registered in previous tax years.

When registering for VAT you need to provide details like your turnover, business activity and bank details.

Your registration date is known as your 'effective date of registration'. You'll have to pay HMRC any VAT due from this date.

You might also need to register in some other cases, depending on the kinds of goods or services you sell and where you sell them.

3. You'll also need to register for VAT if you only sell goods or services that are exempt from VAT or 'out of scope' but you buy goods for more than £85,000 from EU VAT-registered suppliers to use in your business.

4. You may have to register for VAT if you have taken over a VAT-registered business. Check with HMRC on this.

5. There's no threshold if neither you nor your business is based in the UK, and you must register as soon as you supply any goods and services to the UK (or if you expect to in the next 30 days).

Late registration

If you register late, you must pay what you owe from when you should have registered.

You may get a penalty depending on how much you owe and how late your registration is.

6. You can also register voluntarily if your business turnover is below £85,000. You must, however, pay HMRC any VAT you owe from the date they register you.

Getting an exception

You can apply for a registration 'exception' if your taxable turnover goes over the threshold temporarily. You'll need to Write to HMRC with evidence showing why you believe your VAT taxable turnover will not go over the deregistration threshold of £83,000 in the next 12 months.

HMRC will consider your exception and write to confirm if you get one. If not, they will register you for VAT.

Registering for VAT in other EU countries

Usually, you only need to register for VAT where you are based.

Supplying digital services

The rules are different if your business supplies digital services to consumers in other EU countries and those sales go above a certain amount. If in a calendar year (January to December) they go over £8,818 before VAT, you must either:

- register in each country where you are supplying digital services
- sign up for the VAT MOSS service

You need to do this even if your turnover is below the VAT registration threshold.

Digital services include things like broadcasting, telecommunications services, video on demand, downloadable music, games, apps, software and ebooks.

What you can do while you wait for your VAT registration to be confirmed?

Well, you cannot charge or show VAT on your invoices until you get your VAT number. However, you will still have to pay the VAT to HMRC for this period. You should increase your prices to allow for this and tell your customers why. Once you've got your VAT number you can then reissue the invoices showing the VAT.

Your VAT registration certificate

When your registration is successful, you will be sent a VAT registration certificate. This confirms:

- your VAT number
- when to submit your first VAT Return and payment
- your 'effective date of registration' - this depends on the date you went over the threshold, or is the date you asked to register if it was voluntary

You should get your VAT registration certificate within 30 working days, though it can take longer.

It is sent either:

- to your VAT online account
- by post - if an agent registers you or you cannot register online

Claiming Pre-registration VAT

You can reclaim the VAT you have paid on certain purchases made before you registered.

There is, however, a time limit for backdating claims for VAT paid before registration. From your date of registration, the time limit is:

- 4 years for goods you still have, or that were used to make other goods you still have
- 6 months for services

You can only reclaim VAT on purchases for the business now registered for VAT. They must relate to your 'business purpose'. This means they must relate to VAT taxable goods or services that you supply.

You should reclaim them on your first VAT Return (add them to your Box 4 figure) and keep records including:

- invoices and receipts
- a description and purchase dates
- information about how they relate to your business now

Responsibilities of VAT registered businesses

As a VAT registered business, you need to do these six things from your effective date of registration:

1. Charge VAT to all customers at the correct rate
2. Issue invoices and receipts that follow VAT rules
3. Keep a VAT account
4. Send HMRC VAT returns online, on time
5. Pay their VAT as soon as it becomes due
6. Keep all business VAT records

Business records should be kept for 6 years. Examples of business records include:

- Annual accounts, including profit and loss account
- Computer records, emails, stored documents
- Bank statements and paying in slips
- Cash books and other account books

- Credit or debit notes issued or received

- Orders and delivery notes

- Purchase and sales day books

- Purchase invoices and copy sales invoices

- Records of daily takings such as till rolls

- Relevant business correspondence

- Documents from trade with EC member states

- Import and export documents

Most VAT registered businesses that earn over £85,000 must also follow the rules for 'Making Tax Digital for VAT'.

The primary aim of Making Tax Digital is to make tax administration more effective, efficient, and easier for taxpayers through the implementation of a fully digitalised tax system by 2020, whilst also reducing HMRC's overheads for managing tax affairs.

The changes apply to a wide range of taxpayers, including most businesses, self-employed professionals, and landlords. This 'new and improved' tax system will require most business owners to maintain digital records using compatible software.

Once your business is VAT registered, each month or quarter you must produce and reconcile your VAT Return. It is important that you submit the correct values to HMRC.

Rates of VAT and VAT Schemes

There are 3 taxable rates of VAT (20%, 5% & 0%), but some supplies are exempt from VAT and others could be outside the scope of VAT. An exhaustive list of the rates can be found at https://www.gov.uk/vat-rates. If you are unsure about the VAT rate for a specific supply of goods or services, call the VAT Customs & Excise helpline for help, their number is **0300 200 3700,** Text phone **0300 200 3719,** If you are calling from outside the UK, the number **is +44 2920 501 261.** You will need your VAT registration number and postcode, and the figure on box five of one of your latest VAT submitted returns. If you are not VAT registered, you will need your postcode.

Opening times:

8am to 6pm, Monday to Friday

Closed weekends and bank holidays

VAT Schemes

There are three common VAT schemes in use in the UK: Standard accounting scheme, Cash accounting scheme and Flat rate scheme (cash based & invoice based)

a. Standard accounting scheme

For the standard method of accounting, VAT is due in the **tax period** in which the **tax point** can be either basic or actual

Basic Tax point	Actual Tax point
For goods: When the goods are sent to the customer, the customer takes them away, or the goods are available for the customer use.	The date you issue an invoice or receive payment before a basic tax point, **whichever happens first**
For Services: The date that the service being performed is completed.	The invoice date if you issue an invoice up to 14 days after a basic tax point

b. Cash accounting scheme

This scheme allows you to account for output tax on your sales when you receive payment, rather than when you issue the tax invoices. However, you can only reclaim the input tax once you pay your supplier

c. Flat rate scheme

This scheme takes some of the work out of recording VAT sales and purchases by allowing you to apply a single percentage to your turnover in a VAT period.

With the Flat Rate Scheme:

- you pay a fixed rate of VAT over to HMRC

- you keep the difference between what you charge your customers and pay over to HMRC

You cannot reclaim Input Tax when using the flat rate scheme, except for pre-registration expenses and capital purchases over £2,000

You can join the Flat Rate Scheme if:

- you're a VAT-registered business
- you expect your VAT taxable turnover to be £150,000 or less (excluding VAT) in the next 12 months

Flat rate scheme can either be invoice based (whereby you pay VAT based on VAT invoices raised) or cash based (here you calculate VAT based on the turnover received in cash)

The main benefit of the flat rate scheme is the time saved recording VAT on sales and purchases and can also take some of the stress out of completing VAT returns at the quarter end. Because you can easily calculate how much VAT you owe on takings, it can also help in managing cash flow.

How to join the flat rate scheme

You can join the scheme online when you register for VAT.

You can also fill in VAT600 FRS and either:

- email it to frsapplications.vrs@hmrc.gsi.gov.uk
- send it by post to the address on the form

Exceptions

You cannot use the scheme if:

- you left the scheme in the last 12 months
- you committed a VAT offence in the last 12 months, for example VAT evasion
- you joined (or were eligible to join) a VAT group in the last 24 months
- you registered for VAT as a business division in the last 24 months
- your business is closely associated with another business
- you've joined a margin or capital goods VAT scheme

You cannot use the scheme with the Cash Accounting Scheme. Instead, the Flat Rate Scheme has its own cash-based method for calculating the turnover.

Use VAT600 AA/FRS to apply for the Annual Accounting Scheme at the same time.

You will get confirmation you have joined the scheme through your VAT online account (or in the post if you do not apply online).

How to leave

You can choose to leave the scheme at any time. You must leave if;

- you are no longer eligible to be in it
- on the anniversary of joining, your turnover in the last 12 months was more than £230,000 (including VAT) - or you expect it to be in the next 12 months
- you expect your total income in the next 30 days alone to be more than £230,000 (including VAT)

To leave, write to HMRC and they will confirm your leaving date. You must wait 12 months before you can rejoin the scheme again.

HM Revenue and Customs
Imperial House
77 Victoria Street
Grimsby
Lincolnshire
DN31 1DB

How to work out VAT

To work out how much VAT to add to an amount that does not include VAT, multiply the net amount by the percentage of the VAT rate you need to use.

For example, £150 (net) x 20% = £30 VAT to add to £150 to give £180 (gross amount)

To work out how much VAT there is in an amount you have paid that includes VAT, use the VAT fraction for VAT rate used. The VAT fractions are: 1/6 (standard rate) and 1/21 (Reduced rate).

For example: £150 x 1/6 = £25.00 standard rate VAT included in £150, £150 x 1/21 = £7.14 reduced rate VAT included in £150

The VAT fraction is calculated using the formula: VAT rate/(VAT rate + 100). Thus for standard rate, it will be 20/(20+100) which results in 1/6.

Input and Output tax

Inputs are the goods and services which come into the business that are paid for by the business. Any VAT the business pays on inputs is called **input tax, also known as sales tax**.

Outputs are the goods or services that the business sells to customers. The VAT the business adds to these sales is called **output tax, also known as purchase tax**

If you want to remember if something is an input or an output, think about which way the supply of goods or services is moving through the business. Inputs come into the business; Outputs go out.

VAT invoices

Full VAT invoices should show the following items of information:

✓   The name, address and VAT number of your business

✓ A unique reference number for the invoice

✓ Date of the sale and the tax point

✓ A short description of the goods sold, quantity sold, price per single item, total value of the sale for those items (not including VAT), and the VAT rate that applies

✓ The total amount without VAT, the total VAT charged, and the total amount payable

Sample VAT Invoice (detailed)

Tower Chartered Accountants
25 Canada Square
Canary Wharf, London
E14 5LQ
VAT Registration Number   Invoice Number 000787
GB123456789

Invoice Date 06/03/2015

Invoice to:
Kilmorie Capital Ltd
22 Firs road
London
SE23 1BB

Qty	Description	Rate	Net Amount
1	Yearend accounts preparation	1,500	1,500
1	Payroll service for Tax month 11	250	250
		Subtotal	1,750
		VAT @ 20%	350
		Total Amount Payable	2,100

Payment due within 14 days of invoice date. Thanks for your custom

Less detailed invoices can be issued if sales below £250 are regularly made. Less detailed invoices must show the following items of information:

- Your business's name, address, and VAT number
- A short description of the sale, the total price for each item, and the VAT rate
- Date of sale
- The total amount paid
- The total VAT paid

What is a VAT Account and what is it used for?

As mentioned earlier, registered businesses must:

- ✓ collect VAT by adding it to the amounts charged to customers for most goods and services, but can
- ✓ offset against this the VAT that they have been charged by their suppliers
- ✓ pay the VAT balance to Her Majesty's Revenue and Customs (HMRC) – or get a refund if they are owed VAT.

To do this the VAT amounts must be kept separate from the business income and expenditure. This is carried out by maintaining a VAT control account in the main ledger.

The VAT control account records all the VAT on both sales (outputs) and purchases (inputs) so that the balance on the account shows the amount that should be paid to (or claimed from) HMRC.

The details of the business's transactions and the related VAT are recorded on a VAT return, which is sent to HMRC. This is usually carried out every quarter as mentioned earlier on.

The information on the VAT return should agree with the amounts recorded in the VAT control account.

You must keep a VAT account by law. There should be a VAT account for every VAT return period (usually three months).

Here is why it is very useful to keep a VAT account:

a. It shows HMRC how you have worked out the figures you put on the online VAT return form

b. It shows any corrections or adjustments you have made

c. It links the business records to your VAT return

Notes

PREPARING A VAT RETURN

Overview

You usually submit a VAT Return to HM Revenue and Customs (HMRC) every 3 months. This period of time is known as your 'accounting period.'

The VAT Return records things for the accounting period like:

- your total sales and purchases
- the amount of VAT you owe
- the amount of VAT you can reclaim
- what your VAT refund from HMRC is

You must submit a VAT Return even if you have no VAT to pay or reclaim.

Working out what you can claim

If your business is a charity, you pay VAT at a reduced rate of 5% on some goods and services such as:

- residential accommodation (for example, a children's home or care home for the elderly)
- charitable non-business activities (for example, free day care for disabled people)
- small-scale use (up to 1,000 kilowatt hours of electricity a month or a delivery of 2,300 litres of gas oil)

If less than 60% of the fuel and power is for something that qualifies, you'll pay the reduced rate of VAT on the qualifying part and the standard rate (20%) on the rest.
Qualifying fuel and power includes gases, electricity, oils and solid fuels (such as coal). It does not include vehicle fuel.

VAT-registered businesses can usually reclaim the VAT they've paid on business purchases and expenses. The claim must be for a business activity (you have to work out the business element if it also had a personal use).

You must keep records to support your claim and show the VAT was paid.

The exceptions

You cannot reclaim the VAT on:
- entertainment expenses
- purchases if you use the VAT Flat Rate Scheme (except some capital assets worth more than £2,000)

There are special rules for working out how to reclaim VAT for:
- cars, for example buying, repairing, fuel costs
- staff travel expenses, for example accommodation and transport expenses
- businesses that are partly exempt from VAT

Use of estimated figures

Ask HM Revenue and Customs (HMRC) for permission to use estimated figures. You will need a good reason why you cannot give accurate figures on your VAT Return.

If HMRC gives you the permission, you will not be charged a penalty unless you miss the deadline or make a careless or deliberate error. You will normally have to give the correct figures in your next VAT Return.

Bad debt relief

You can reclaim the VAT you have paid HMRC but not received from a customer if it's a 'bad debt' (one you've written off). To qualify for the relief:
- the debt must be between 6 months old and 4 years and 6 months old
- you must not have sold the debt on
- you must not have charged more than the normal price for the item

You should reclaim them via your VAT Return (add them to your Box 4 figure) and keep records about the debt.

If the debt is paid, you must pay the relief back via your VAT Return by adding the amount to your 'Box 1' figure.

How to submit your VAT return

You must submit your return online unless:
- your business is subject to an insolvency procedure - if you have a Company Voluntary Arrangement or an Individual Voluntary Arrangement you can submit your return online if you want to
- you object to using computers on religious grounds
- you cannot because of your age, a disability or because of where you live, for example you do not have internet access

Contact HM Revenue and Customs (HMRC) to find out how to submit your return, for example paper filing, if you cannot submit online.

To Submit a VAT Return to HMRC, you need a VAT number and a VAT online account. You can then submit your VAT Return using HMRC's free online service or commercial accounting software. You cannot use your online account to send your VAT Return if you have signed up for 'Making Tax Digital for VAT'. Use compatible accounting software instead.

A list of commercial software providers can be found by clicking here or by visiting this link; https://www.gov.uk/government/publications/vat-returns-and-ec-sales-list-commercial-software-suppliers/vat-commercial-software-suppliers

How to prepare a VAT Return in five steps

There is a 5 –step process of completing a VAT return and the VAT return should be sent to HMRC for every tax period. A tax period is usually three months. Any payment of VAT that is due should reach HMRC by the due date, which should be shown on the online VAT return and online VAT return acknowledgement.

Step by step process:

Step 1
Gather your business records. These will include getting together all financial documents and records for the period of the return. These records will include petty cash records, purchase and sales invoices and any credit notes and any bad debts written off

Step 2
Now, use these business records to create a VAT account for the period as shown below (use real figures to replace X in the debit & credit columns

Box	Entries	Debit	Credit
4	VAT from payments in the petty cash book	X	
4	VAT from invoices in the purchases daybook	X	
4	VAT from credit notes in the purchases returns daybook	X	
1	VAT from cash sales receipts in the cash book		X
1	VAT from invoices in the sales daybook		X
1	VAT from credit notes in the sales returns daybook	X	
1	VAT from irrecoverable debt written off in journal		X
4	VAT from cash payments in the cash book	X	
5	Balancing figure*		
	Totals (Total Debits should equal Total Credits)	XX	XX

The balancing figure (number 5) in the table above will either be a repayment to the business (if the sum of the number 4's is more than the sum of the number 1's) or a payment that the business needs to make to HMRC (if the sum of the number 1's is more than the sum of the number 4's)If it is a repayment, put the value on the credit side, and if it is a payment, put the value on the debit side.

Step 3

Make sure that the figures in the VAT account above are accurate by doing the following VAT checklist

Step	Description	Tick
a	Has all output tax been traced to sales invoices or Daily Income sheets and invoices?	☐
b	Has all output tax been declared at the correct VAT rate?	☐
c	Has all input tax been traced to purchase invoices and petty cash vouchers?	☐
d	Has all input tax been claimed at the correct VAT rate?	☐
e	Have all bank receipt and bank payment entries been checked to ensure that the correct VAT code has been applied?	☐
f	Have all bad debts been entered onto the accounting system and the VAT claimed?	☐
g	Have sales invoices been issued for any asset sales? Has the correct output tax been declared?	☐
h	Check that no input tax has been claimed for goods for private use	☐
i	Check that input tax has not been claimed for entertainment (unless it can be proven to be wholly and exclusively a business cost)	☐
j	Has a fuel scale charge been included in the VAT calculation (needed if the company pays ANY private petrol/diesel bills)?	☐
k	Has only 50% of the input VAT been claimed on any cars that are leased or hired?	☐

l	If you make exempt supplies have you checked whether the partial exemption rules apply?	☐
m	If you import or export goods have all the documentation been kept and recorded and treated correctly for VAT purposes?	☐
n	If you have dealt with firms in other countries have you recorded their VAT registration numbers?	☐
o	Has the nominal code for VAT been checked to ensure that no journals have been entered which would affect the VAT return?	☐
p	Have all manual additions been checked?	☐

Step 4

Once the checklist is done, use the figures in the VAT account above to establish the following:

  a. VAT due in this period for sales (sum figure of boxes labelled 1 in VAT account above)
  b. Vat reclaimed in this period on purchases (sum figure of boxes labelled 4 in VAT account above)

In addition to a & b above, you will also need to verify the

  c. The total value of sales excluding VAT
  d. Total value of purchases excluding VAT

You will use these figures later to fill out the online VAT return.

Step 5

Submit the VAT Return to HMRC. Please note that you need to have already enrolled for this service by registering or HMRC online Taxes (VAT)

Complete and send your VAT Return online.

Remember, you cannot use your online account to send your VAT Return if you have signed up for 'Making Tax Digital for VAT'. Use compatible accounting software instead.

Notes

To Submit a VAT Return to HMRC, you need a VAT number and a VAT online account. You can then submit your VAT Return using HMRC's free online service or commercial accounting software.

You cannot use your online account to send your VAT Return if you have signed up for 'Making Tax Digital for VAT'. Use compatible accounting software instead.

FILING A VAT RETURN USING HMRC FREE SOFTWARE

Once you have your figures ready from the five steps in the previous chapter, log into your HMRC VAT online account to start the process of submitting the return to HMRC.

If you are using commercial software, you don't have to follow this procedure, check out subsequent chapters for the way to do that (Sage 50, Xero and QuickBooks online). Most accounting software lets you submit your VAT Return to HMRC directly. This means you will not have to enter your figures separately in HMRC's online service.
HMRC has a list of software you can use to submit your VAT Return.

Getting online

If you need:
- a VAT number and online account - register for VAT
- an online account - sign up for an online account and select 'VAT submit returns'
- a VAT number - log in to your online account and apply for a VAT number

HMRC's free online service

Now, proceeding with the submission using HMRC free software, type in https://www.gov.uk/log-in-register-hmrc-online-services on to your internet browser and a window similar to the figure on the next page will appear.

Fig. 1

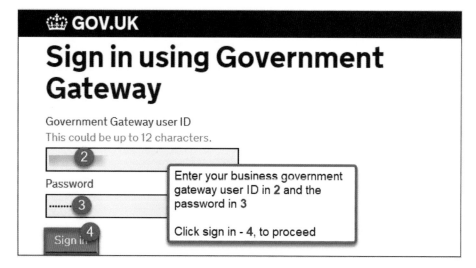

Fig. 2

Fig. 3

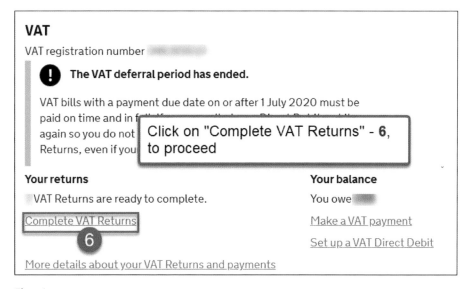

Fig. 4

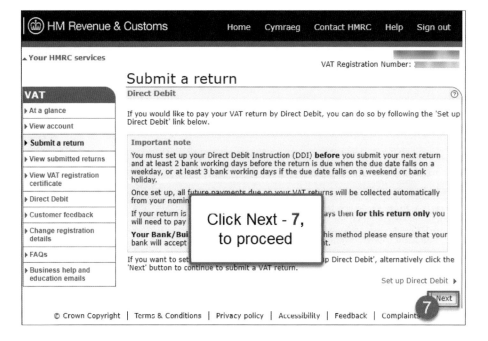

Fig. 5

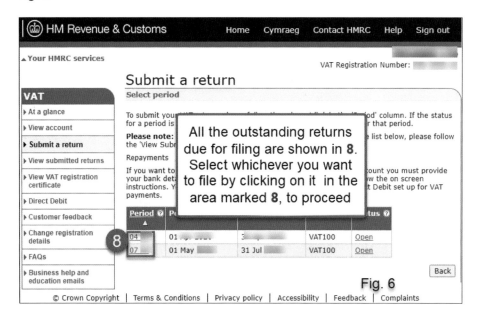

Fig. 6

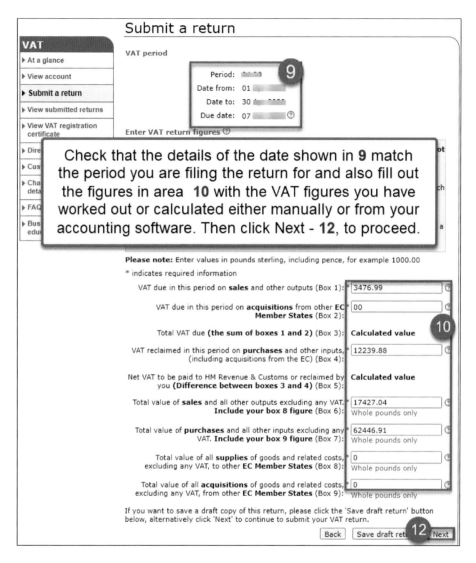

Submit a return

VAT

▶ At a glance

▶ View account

▶ **Submit a return**

▶ View submitted returns

▶ View VAT registration certificate

▶ Dire

▶ Cus

▶ Cha deta

▶ FAQ

▶ Bus edu

VAT period

Period:

Date from: 01

Date to: 30

Due date: 07

Enter VAT return figures

> Check that the details of the date shown in **9** match the period you are filing the return for and also fill out the figures in area **10** with the VAT figures you have worked out or calculated either manually or from your accounting software. Then click Next - **12**, to proceed.

Please note: Enter values in pounds sterling, including pence, for example 1000.00

* indicates required information

VAT due in this period on **sales** and other outputs (Box 1):	3476.99
VAT due in this period on **acquisitions** from other **EC Member States** (Box 2):	00
Total VAT due **(the sum of boxes 1 and 2)** (Box 3):	**Calculated value**
VAT reclaimed in this period on **purchases** and other inputs, (including acquisitions from the EC) (Box 4):	12239.88
Net VAT to be paid to HM Revenue & Customs or reclaimed by you **(Difference between boxes 3 and 4)** (Box 5):	**Calculated value**
Total value of **sales** and all other outputs excluding any VAT. **Include your box 8 figure** (Box 6):	17427.04 Whole pounds only
Total value of **purchases** and all other inputs excluding any VAT. **Include your box 9 figure** (Box 7):	62446.91 Whole pounds only
Total value of all **supplies** of goods and related costs, excluding any VAT, to other **EC Member States** (Box 8):	0 Whole pounds only
Total value of all **acquisitions** of goods and related costs, excluding any VAT, from other **EC Member States** (Box 9):	0 Whole pounds only

If you want to save a draft copy of this return, please click the 'Save draft return' button below, alternatively click 'Next' to continue to submit your VAT return.

[Back] [Save draft ret] [Next]

Fig. 7

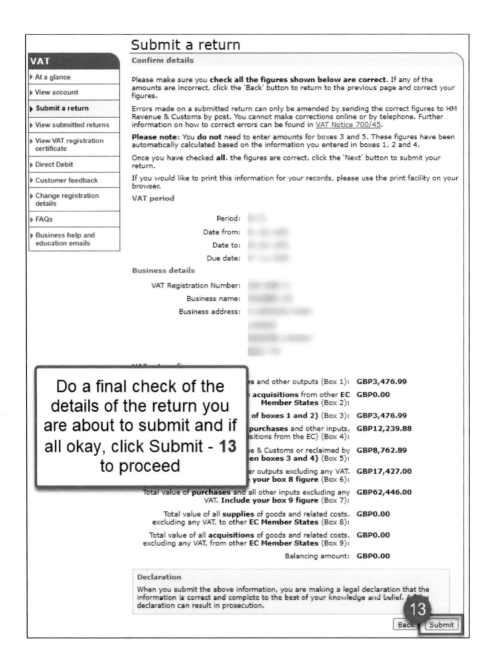

Submit a return

Confirm details

VAT

▶ At a glance
▶ View account
▶ **Submit a return**
▶ View submitted returns
▶ View VAT registration certificate
▶ Direct Debit
▶ Customer feedback
▶ Change registration details
▶ FAQs
▶ Business help and education emails

Please make sure you **check all the figures shown below are correct**. If any of the amounts are incorrect, click the 'Back' button to return to the previous page and correct your figures.

Errors made on a submitted return can only be amended by sending the correct figures to HM Revenue & Customs by post. You cannot make corrections online or by telephone. Further information on how to correct errors can be found in VAT Notice 700/45.

Please note: You **do not** need to enter amounts for boxes 3 and 5. These figures have been automatically calculated based on the information you entered in boxes 1, 2 and 4.

Once you have checked **all**. the figures are correct, click the 'Next' button to submit your return.

If you would like to print this information for your records, please use the print facility on your browser.

VAT period

Period:
Date from:
Date to:
Due date:

Business details

VAT Registration Number:
Business name:
Business address:

Do a final check of the details of the return you are about to submit and if all okay, click Submit - **13** to proceed

...s and other outputs (Box 1): GBP3,476.99
...acquisitions from other EC Member States (Box 2): GBP0.00
...of boxes 1 and 2) (Box 3): GBP3,476.99
...purchases and other inputs, ...sitions from the EC) (Box 4): GBP12,239.88
...e & Customs or reclaimed by ...en boxes 3 and 4) (Box 5): GBP8,762.89
...er outputs excluding any VAT. ...your box 8 figure (Box 6): GBP17,427.00

Total value of **purchases** and all other inputs excluding any VAT. **Include your box 9 figure** (Box 7): GBP62,446.00

Total value of all **supplies** of goods and related costs, excluding any VAT, to other **EC Member States** (Box 8): GBP0.00

Total value of all **acquisitions** of goods and related costs, excluding any VAT, from other **EC Member States** (Box 9): GBP0.00

Balancing amount: GBP0.00

Declaration

When you submit the above information, you are making a legal declaration that the information is correct and complete to the best of your knowledge and belief. A false declaration can result in prosecution.

Back | Submit

13

Figure 8.

Remember to keep any reference number you receive as proof to show that you have sent your return.

That is how to submit a VAT Return using HMRC Free software.

Notes

Notes

PREPARING AND FILING A VAT RETURN USING SAGE 50 ACCOUNTS

Pre-processing checklist

Before starting your VAT return process, it is always important to go through the VAT return checklist (see below, making sure that everything has been done)

Step	Description	Tick
i	Has all output tax been traced to sales invoices or Daily Income sheets and invoices?	☐
ii	Has all output tax been declared at the correct VAT rate?	☐
iii	Has all input tax been traced to purchase invoices and petty cash vouchers?	☐
iv	Has all input tax been claimed at the correct VAT rate?	☐
v	Have all bank receipt and bank payment entries been checked to ensure that the correct VAT code has been applied?	☐
vi	Have all bad debts been entered onto the accounting system and the VAT claimed?	☐
vii	Have sales invoices been issued for any asset sales? Has the correct output tax been declared?	☐
viii	Check that no input tax has been claimed for goods for private use	☐

ix	Check that input tax has not been claimed for entertainment (unless it can be proven to be wholly and exclusively a business cost)	☐
x	Has a fuel scale charge been included in the VAT calculation (needed if the company pays ANY private petrol/diesel bills)?	☐
xi	Has only 50% of the input VAT been claimed on any cars that are leased or hired?	☐
xii	If you make exempt supplies have you checked whether the partial exemption rules apply?	☐
xiii	If you import or export goods have all the documentation been kept and recorded and treated correctly for VAT purposes?	☐
xiv	If you have dealt with firms in other countries have you recorded their VAT registration numbers?	☐
xv	Has the nominal code for VAT been checked to ensure that no journals have been entered which would affect the VAT return?	☐
xvi	Have all manual additions been checked?	☐

After successfully going through the checklist above, proceed with the VAT return process set up as below.

Calculating the VAT Return doesn't affect your transactions in Sage Accounts, no postings are made to your nominal codes. This means that you can calculate your VAT Return as many times as necessary. However, when you mark your transactions as being reconciled, this prevents them from being automatically included in a future VAT return calculated in Sage Accounts.

Preparation:

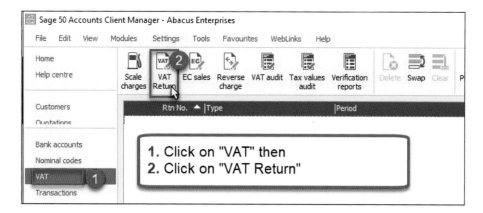

Fig. 9

A VAT Return window appears after step 2 in the figure above. See figure 200 in the next page.

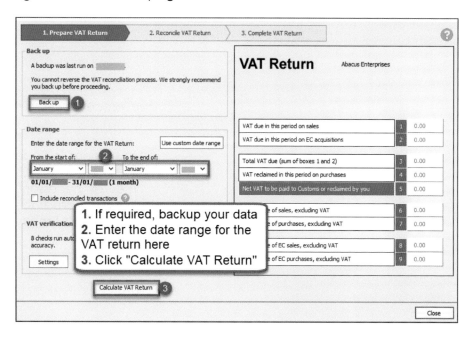

Fig. 10

When you click on "Calculate VAT Return" – step 3 as illustrated in the figure above, if there are any transactions dated before the date range (Step 2 as illustrated in the figure above) which haven't been reconciled, the earlier reconciled transactions window appears.

To include these transactions, click OK, if you don't want to include these transactions, click ignore

If, however there are no transactions dated before the date range selected, a figure similar to the window below will appear.

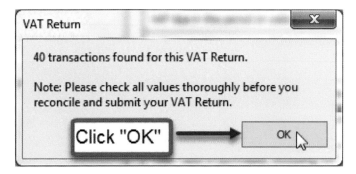

Fig. 11

After you click OK as illustrated in the figure above, you then move to the reconciliation window

Reconciliation:

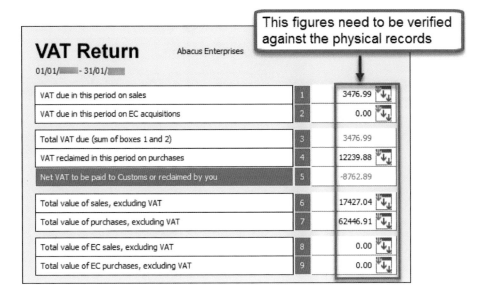

Fig. 12

A brief note about VAT returns

You usually submit a VAT Return to HM Revenue and Customs (HMRC) every 3 months. This period of time is known as your 'accounting period.'

The VAT Return records things for the accounting period like:

- ✓ *your total sales and purchases*
- ✓ *the amount of VAT you owe*
- ✓ *the amount of VAT you can reclaim*
- ✓ *what your VAT refund from HMRC is*

You must submit a VAT Return even if you have no VAT to pay or reclaim.

Final VAT Returns

You have to submit a final VAT Return when you cancel your VAT registration. You can usually do this online using your VAT online account.

Reconciling the figures to the source documents:

Click on the three down facing arrows in box 1 (at the right of box 1) and a VAT Breakdown window will appear – see figure below

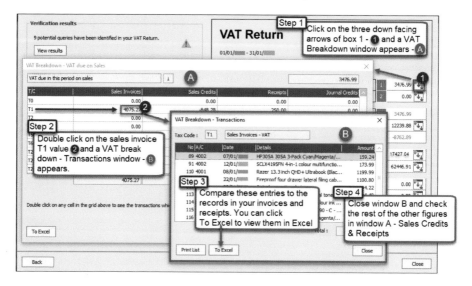

Fig. 13

You will need to check and reconcile all the figures in windows B (as illustrated in the figure above) to the original source documents and do the same for figures in box 4, 6, 7, 8 and 9 of the VAT Return as well.

After checking the figures in each box (1-9) remember to close the excel document, window B and window A.

If you require to make any adjustments to any values of the VAT return, see inset instruction as illustrated in the figure on the next page.

Only follow instructions in figure 14 on the next page if you have some adjustments to make otherwise just go to figure 15 for the next steps in the VAT return preparation

PREPARING AND FILING A VAT RETURN USING SAGE 50 ACCOUNTS

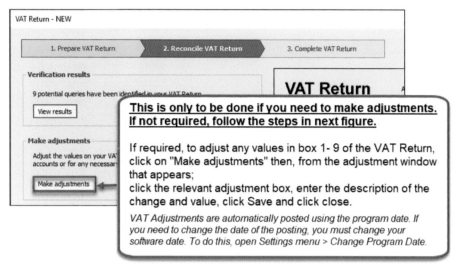

Fig. 14

Final step in Reconciliation:

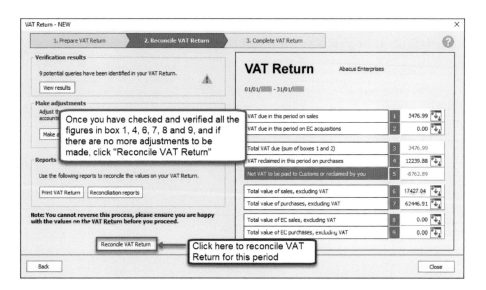

Fig. 15

Once you click on "Reconcile VAT Return" as illustrated in the figure above, a confirmation window appears – see below.

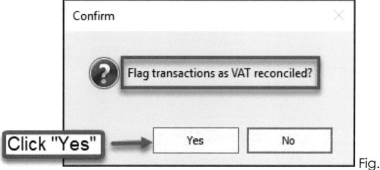

Fig. 16

Once you click Yes as illustrated in the figure above, the reconciliation progress bar appears and the eventually a reconciled VAT return is displayed. See figure below.

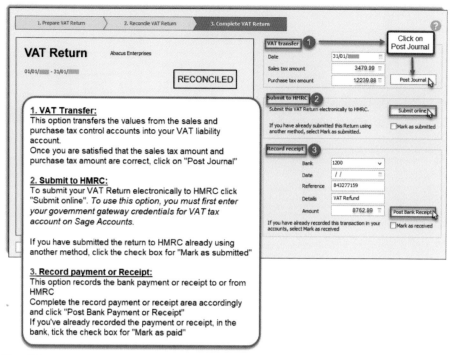

Fig. 17

PREPARING AND FILING A VAT RETURN USING SAGE 50 ACCOUNTS

Printing the VAT reports:

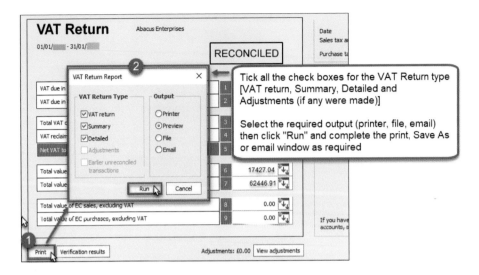

Fig. 18

Please note that once you have reconciled your VAT Return, it isn't possible to undo a VAT reconciliation. To correct this, you need to restore a backup taken before the VAT Return was reconciled.

Notes

You usually submit a VAT Return to HM Revenue and Customs (HMRC) every 3 months. This period of time is known as your 'accounting period.'

PREPARING AND FILING A VAT RETURN USING QUICKBOOKS ONLINE

Pre-processing checklist

Before starting your VAT return process, it is always important to go through the VAT return checklist (see below, making sure that everything has been done)

Step	Description	Tick
i	Has all output tax been traced to sales invoices or Daily Income sheets and invoices?	☐
ii	Has all output tax been declared at the correct VAT rate?	☐
iii	Has all input tax been traced to purchase invoices and petty cash vouchers?	☐
iv	Has all input tax been claimed at the correct VAT rate?	☐
v	Have all bank receipt and bank payment entries been checked to ensure that the correct VAT code has been applied?	☐
vi	Have all bad debts been entered onto the accounting system and the VAT claimed?	☐
vii	Have sales invoices been issued for any asset sales? Has the correct output tax been declared?	☐
viii	Check that no input tax has been claimed for goods for private use	☐

ix	Check that input tax has not been claimed for entertainment (unless it can be proven to be wholly and exclusively a business cost)	☐
x	Has a fuel scale charge been included in the VAT calculation (needed if the company pays ANY private petrol/diesel bills)?	☐
xi	Has only 50% of the input VAT been claimed on any cars that are leased or hired?	☐
xii	If you make exempt supplies have you checked whether the partial exemption rules apply?	☐
xiii	If you import or export goods have all the documentation been kept and recorded and treated correctly for VAT purposes?	☐
xiv	If you have dealt with firms in other countries have you recorded their VAT registration numbers?	☐
xv	Has the nominal code for VAT been checked to ensure that no journals have been entered which would affect the VAT return?	☐
xvi	Have all manual additions been checked?	☐

After successfully going through the checklist above, proceed with the VAT return process set up as below.

Calculating the VAT Return does not affect your transactions in QuickBooks online, no postings are made to your nominal codes. This means that you can calculate your VAT Return as many times as necessary. However, when you mark your transactions as being reconciled, this prevents them from being automatically included in a future VAT return calculated in QuickBooks online.

Preparation:

Fig. 19

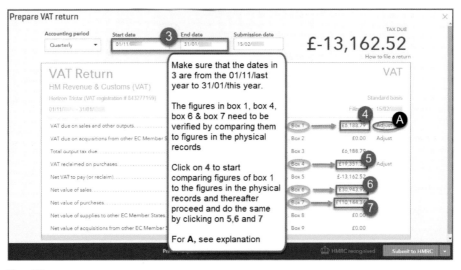

Fig. 20

If you have discovered any mismatch (errors) in the figures in this return, please go to the transactions and amend them.

If you need to make any adjustment to this return due to errors in previous VAT returns that were discovered after the VAT return(s) was submitted, click on Adjust – **A,** to adjust the figures in box 1 or 4.

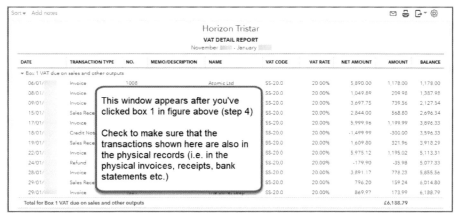

Fig. 21

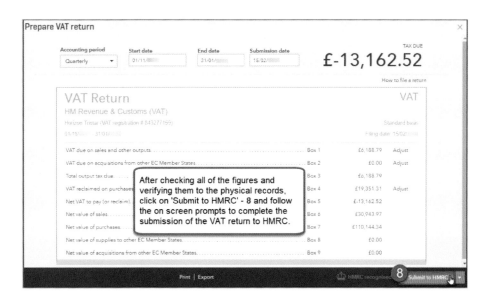

Fig. 22

PREPARING AND FILING A VAT RETURN USING XERO

Pre-processing checklist

Before starting your VAT return process, it is always important to go through the VAT return checklist (see below, making sure that everything has been done)

Step	Description	Tick
i	Has all output tax been traced to sales invoices or Daily Income sheets and invoices?	☐
ii	Has all output tax been declared at the correct VAT rate?	☐
iii	Has all input tax been traced to purchase invoices and petty cash vouchers?	☐
iv	Has all input tax been claimed at the correct VAT rate?	☐
v	Have all bank receipt and bank payment entries been checked to ensure that the correct VAT code has been applied?	☐
vi	Have all bad debts been entered onto the accounting system and the VAT claimed?	☐
vii	Have sales invoices been issued for any asset sales? Has the correct output tax been declared?	☐
viii	Check that no input tax has been claimed for goods for private use	☐

ix	Check that input tax has not been claimed for entertainment (unless it can be proven to be wholly and exclusively a business cost)	☐
x	Has a fuel scale charge been included in the VAT calculation (needed if the company pays ANY private petrol/diesel bills)?	☐
xi	Has only 50% of the input VAT been claimed on any cars that are leased or hired?	☐
xii	If you make exempt supplies have you checked whether the partial exemption rules apply?	☐
xiii	If you import or export goods have all the documentation been kept and recorded and treated correctly for VAT purposes?	☐
xiv	If you have dealt with firms in other countries have you recorded their VAT registration numbers?	☐
xv	Has the nominal code for VAT been checked to ensure that no journals have been entered which would affect the VAT return?	☐
xvi	Have all manual additions been checked?	☐

After successfully going through the checklist above, proceed with the VAT return process set up as below.

Calculating the VAT Return does not affect your transactions in QuickBooks online, no postings are made to your nominal codes. This means that you can calculate your VAT Return as many times as necessary. However, when you mark your transactions as being reconciled, this prevents them from being automatically included in a future VAT return calculated in QuickBooks online.

PREPARING AND FILING A VAT RETURN USING XERO

Preparation:

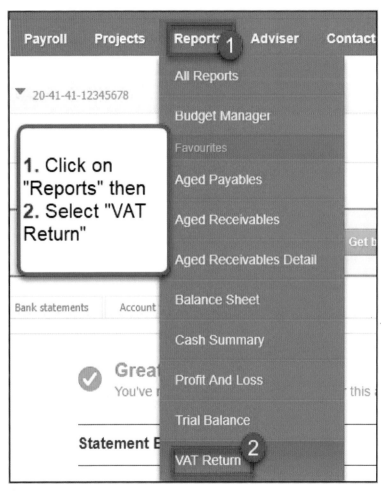

Fig. 23

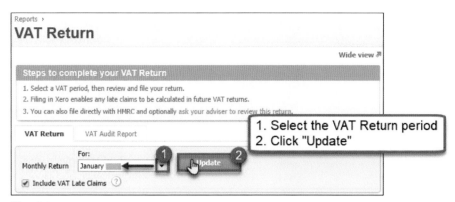

Fig. 24

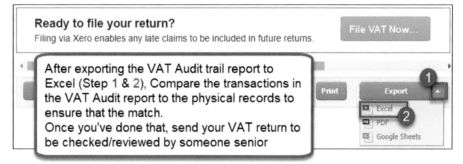

Fig. 25

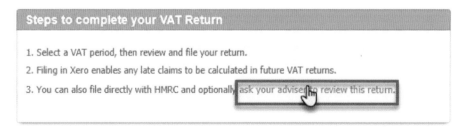

Fig. 26

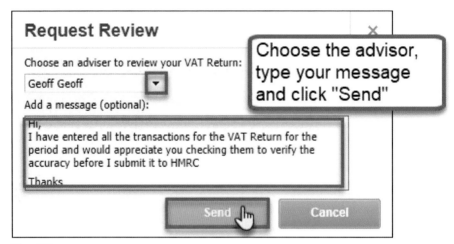

Fig. 27

Once review by your supervisor is done and you are given a go ahead to submit the VAT return to HMRC, click "File VAT Now..." – see below

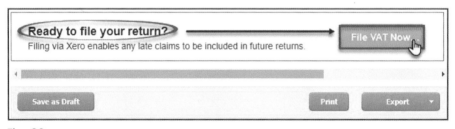

Fig. 28

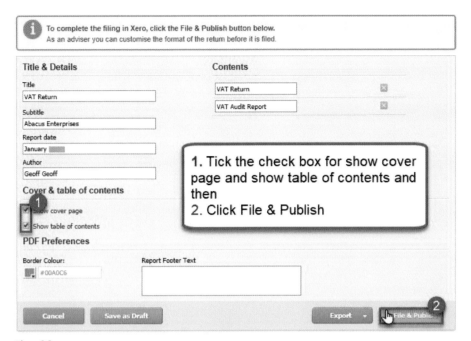

Fig. 29

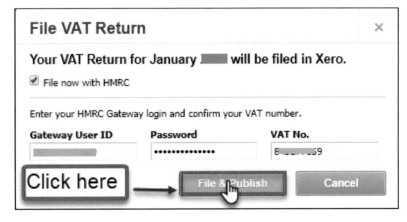

Fig. 30

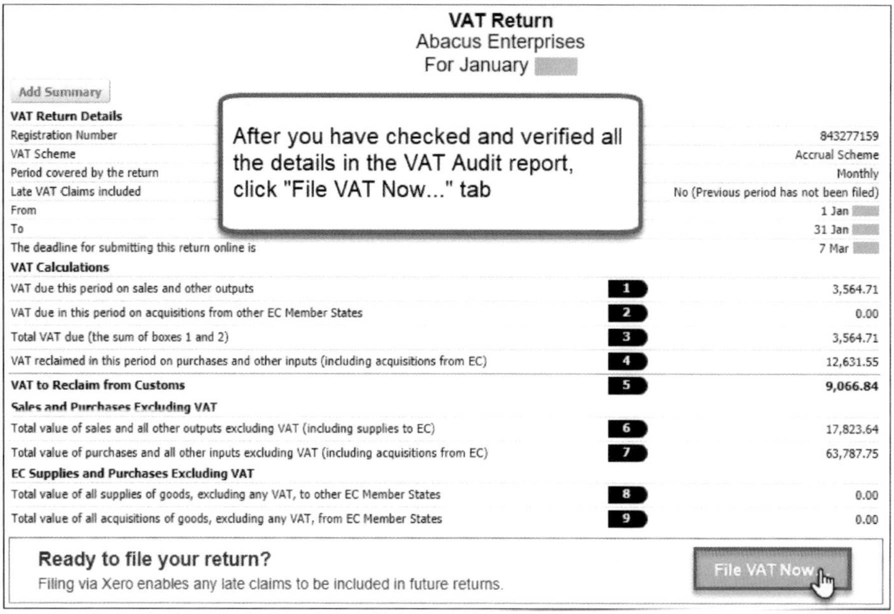

VAT Return
Abacus Enterprises
For January ▨

Add Summary

VAT Return Details

Registration Number	843277159
VAT Scheme	Accrual Scheme
Period covered by the return	Monthly
Late VAT Claims included	No (Previous period has not been filed)
From	1 Jan ▨
To	31 Jan ▨
The deadline for submitting this return online is	7 Mar ▨

> After you have checked and verified all the details in the VAT Audit report, click "File VAT Now..." tab

VAT Calculations

VAT due this period on sales and other outputs	**1**	3,564.71
VAT due in this period on acquisitions from other EC Member States	**2**	0.00
Total VAT due (the sum of boxes 1 and 2)	**3**	3,564.71
VAT reclaimed in this period on purchases and other inputs (including acquisitions from EC)	**4**	12,631.55
VAT to Reclaim from Customs	**5**	**9,066.84**

Sales and Purchases Excluding VAT

Total value of sales and all other outputs excluding VAT (including supplies to EC)	**6**	17,823.64
Total value of purchases and all other inputs excluding VAT (including acquisitions from EC)	**7**	63,787.75

EC Supplies and Purchases Excluding VAT

Total value of all supplies of goods, excluding any VAT, to other EC Member States	**8**	0.00
Total value of all acquisitions of goods, excluding any VAT, from EC Member States	**9**	0.00

Ready to file your return?
Filing via Xero enables any late claims to be included in future returns.

File VAT Now

Fig. 31

Notes

Calculating the VAT Return does not affect your transactions in QuickBooks online, no postings are made to your nominal codes. This means that you can calculate your VAT Return as many times as necessary. However, when you mark your transactions as being reconciled, this prevents them from being automatically included in a future VAT return calculated in QuickBooks online.

CORRECTING MISTAKES IN YOUR VAT RUTURN AFTER YOU HAVE FILED IT TO HMRC

Now, after you have reconciled and submitted your VAT return, you discover later that you made a mistake in the VAT return, what do you do?

Well, don't worry, you can still sort it out.

There are two methods you can use to correct errors but the method you choose will depend on how much the error of VAT is.

Method 1	Method 2
You can use this method to correct the error by adjusting your VAT account and include the value of that adjustment on your current VAT return providing: • the net value of errors found on previous returns does not exceed £10,000, or • the net value of errors found on previous returns is between £10,000 and £50,000 but does not exceed 1% of the box 6 (net outputs) VAT return declaration due for the return period in which the errors are discovered	You must use this method if: • the net value of errors found on previous returns is between £10,000 and £50,000 and exceeds 1% of the box 6 (net outputs) VAT return declaration due for the current return period during which the error was discovered, or • the net value of errors found on previous returns is greater than £50,000 or the errors on previous returns were made deliberately

To work out the net value of VAT errors on previous returns, you should work out:

   • the total amount due to HMRC, if any, and

- the total amount due to you if any

If the difference between the two figures is greater than £10,000 and exceeds 1% of the box 6 value (net outputs) in the VAT return declaration due for the current return period during which the error is discovered, you must use Method 2.

You must always use Method 2 if the net errors exceed £50,000 or if the errors made on previous returns were made deliberately.

You may, if you wish, use method 2 for errors of any size which are below the limits mentioned in method 1, instead of a Method 1 error correction.
If you choose to use method 2 in this case, you must not make adjustment for the same errors on a later VAT return.

Notifying HMRC of an error

Failure to correct errors can result in a penalty and interest. Use form VAT652 to tell HM Revenue and Customs of any errors that you have made on your previous VAT returns that are over the current error reporting threshold.

The form can be accessed, if you have internet access, by going to: https://www.gov.uk/government/publications/vat-notification-of-errors-in-vat-returns-vat-652 and fill out the HMRC online form VAT652

If you have no internet access you can request a form by contacting the VAT Helpline on Telephone: 0300 200 3700.

If you have access to the internet and are able to visit the link above, a window similar to what is on the next page will appear.

Fig. 32

HM Revenue
& Customs

Notification of errors in VAT Returns

About this form

This form is designed to be filled in on screen. You must complete all boxes. You cannot save the form but once you've completed it you'll be able to print a copy and post it.

You can use this form to disclose the details of any errors in your VAT returns. **Please read the notes below before you complete this form.**

Notes

What is this form used for?

When you find you have made an error(s) in a previous VAT return you must tell HM Revenue and Customs (HMRC) and you can use this form to do so. You can include the net value of the adjustment in the VAT return for the period of discovery if the net value of the errors doesn't exceed the greater of:

• £10,000 or

• 1% of the box 6 figure required on the VAT return for the period of discovery, subject to an upper limit of £50,000. If you've included, or intend to include, the adjustment in the VAT return for the period of discovery then you should select 'Yes' in the field marked 'Adjusted in VAT return' to indicate this.

How to use this form

You should enter details separately for each VAT period ('Period reference'). Amounts in Boxes 1 to 5 should be entered in pounds and pence and for Boxes 6 to 9 in pounds only. You will need to manually calculate the difference amounts for Boxes 1 to 5 and select from the drop down menu if the amount is payable to HMRC or repayable to you. If Box 5 is a net repayment due to you please enter a nega[...]ly submitted' and 'Correct figures' boxes.

Click Next - **2**, to proceed

Fig. 33

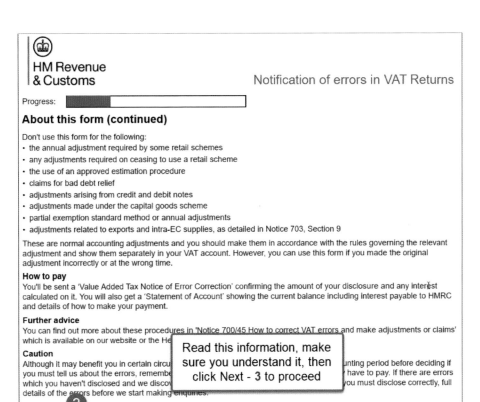

Fig. 34

Notes

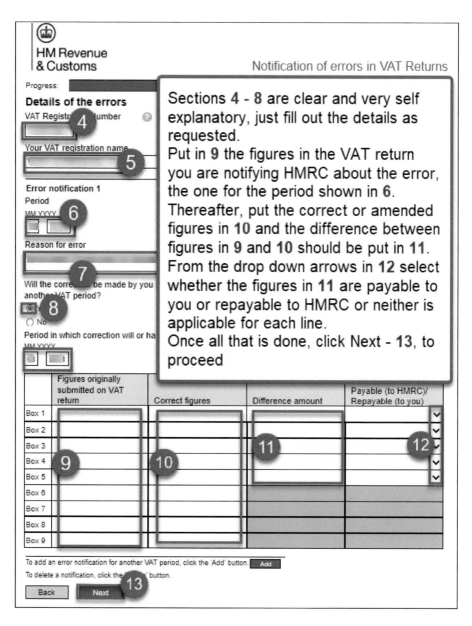

Fig. 35

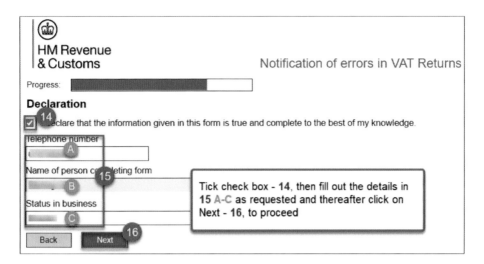

Fig. 36

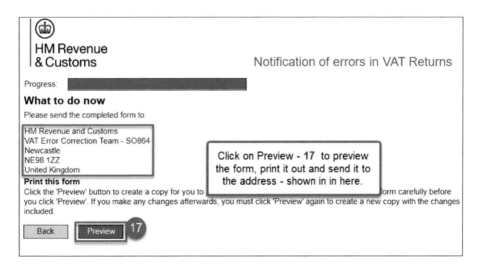

Fig. 37

HOW TO EFFECTIVELY DEAL WITH A VAT INSPECTION

The prospect of a VAT inspection is often a very stressful one for most business owners. It is one of those things that you never know exactly when it might happen. When it happens, HM Revenue and Customs (HMRC) usually will contact you to arrange a visit and they normally give you 7 days' notice.

They'll confirm what information they'll want to see, how long it's likely to take and if
they want to inspect your premises. You can ask them to delay the visit. But,
They can also visit without an appointment and telephone you about your VAT.

When VAT officers visit your business, they often inspect your VAT records and make sure you are paying or reclaiming the right amount of VAT.

How often you get a visit depends on:
- how big or complex your business is
- whether you have submitted late or incorrect VAT Returns before

Well, let us just say you can't help but expect a VAT visit at some point in time if you are VAT registered. So, I have here some things you should do to prepare your business now and be ready to handle any VAT inspection when it happens.

Here is what to do.

Advance preparation

The most obvious step is to ensure your VAT affairs are totally in order. Keep track of input and output VAT and ensure your VAT returns are not late. Even if you feel competent to do this yourself, it is a good investment to pay a professional to take an overview for you is highly recommended – they will ensure you stay within the law.

Have you thought about protection?

I think is worth it for every business taking out VAT investigation insurance. If you are subsequently investigated, the policy will pay an accountant to handle the investigation for you. It can sometimes be very expensive dealing with a VAT inspection if things turn out to be complicated.

Some policies also cover other tax investigations. One of the most cost-effective ways to get this insurance is to join an organisation such as the Forum of Private Business – which, amongst other membership benefits, provides members with tax investigation cover.

Okay, like I said, the question is not if, but when you will receive a visit from the VAT
officers. So, let's look at some of the things to do when it is certain that they are coming.

Book the inspection date down on your calendar

Keep your calendar cleared for that day.

Get Your Staff Ready

Ensure your staff are aware that the business is being investigated and that it is a routine event you are prepared for. There's nothing more worrying than seeing the boss stressed while a stranger looks through the paperwork. It's also worth telling your staff that if the inspector asks them any questions, they should direct them to you rather than attempt to answer them.

On the day of the visit

Get in early, make sure you have your last three years' audited accounts available, and your bookkeeper or accountant is readily available – ideally in person. Be polite and professional when dealing with the VAT Officer. Give them plenty of room to work in and keep them comfortable with tea and coffee as appropriate. But also ensure you stay in control.

During the visit

HMRC will work with you to put right any problems with your VAT. They'll also tell you about any additional tax and penalty you have to pay. Helping them with the check will reduce the amount of any penalty.

It's vital that you or your representative keep careful notes of what is said to you by the VAT Officer. Get copies of their interpretations of VAT law in writing; this will help you apply their ruling consistently and deal with any future challenges.

Stay calm

An investigation won't necessarily find anything wrong, and you do have rights, including the right of appeal. The most extreme option to you is to appeal to a VAT tribunal. A VAT specialist will be able to advise you on this. Don't panic

After the visit

Continue business as usual and wait for HMRC response HMRC will normally write to you confirming:

- what you must do to improve your VAT record keeping if need be

- any corrections you must make to your VAT account if they found out any errors during their visit
- if you're overpaying or underpaying your VAT
- any penalty you have to pay

Like I mentioned earlier, you can appeal an HMRC decision against your business as result of the inspection but you must do it within 30 days.

Getting help

You can get help with your VAT return or if you do not understand something about your tax. Contact the VAT Online Services Helpdesk if you need any help using VAT online services.

Deadlines

Check your VAT Return and payment deadlines in your VAT online account.

Your VAT online account tells you:
- when your VAT Returns are due
- when the payment must clear HM Revenue and Customs' (HMRC) account

The deadline for submitting the return online and paying HMRC are usually the same - 1 calendar month and 7 days after the end of an accounting period. You need to allow time for the payment to reach HMRC's account.

Exceptions

The deadlines are different if, for example, you use the VAT Annual Accounting Scheme.

Paying your VAT bill

You must pay VAT to HMRC electronically, for example through direct debit or internet banking. Most businesses are not allowed to pay by cheque. If you cannot pay your VAT bill, contact HMRC as soon as possible about it.

Notes

The most obvious step is to ensure your VAT affairs are totally in order. Keep track of input and output VAT and ensure your VAT returns are not late. Even if you feel competent to do this yourself, it is a good investment to pay a professional to take an overview for you is highly recommended – they will ensure you stay within the law.

PENALTIES AND SURCHARGES

HM Revenue and Customs (HMRC) record a 'default' if:
- they do not receive your VAT return by the deadline
- full payment for the VAT due on your return has not reached their account by the deadline

VAT Surcharges

You may enter a 12-month 'surcharge period' if you default. If you default again during this time:
- the surcharge period is extended for a further 12 months
- you may have to pay an extra amount (a 'surcharge') on top of the VAT you owe

If you submit a late return, you will not have to pay a surcharge if you:
- pay your VAT in full by the deadline
- have no tax to pay
- are due a VAT repayment

HMRC will write to you explaining any surcharges you owe and what happens if you default again.

How much will you pay?

Your surcharge is a percentage of the VAT outstanding on the due date for the accounting period that is in default. The surcharge rate increases every time you default again in a surcharge period.

This table shows how much you'll be charged if you default within a surcharge period.

You do not pay a surcharge for your first default.

Defaults within 12 months	Surcharge if annual turnover is less than £150,000	Surcharge if annual turnover is £150,000 or more
2nd	No surcharge	2% (no surcharge if this is less than £400)
3rd	2% (no surcharge if this is less than £400)	5% (no surcharge if this is less than £400)
4th	5% (no surcharge if this is less than £400)	10% or £30 (whichever is more)
5th	10% or £30 (whichever is more)	15% or £30 (whichever is more)
6 or more	15% or £30 (whichever is more)	15% or £30 (whichever is more)

Penalties

HMRC can charge you a penalty of up to:
- 100% of any tax under-stated or over-claimed if you send a return that contains a careless or deliberate inaccuracy
- 30% of an assessment if HMRC sends you one that's too low and you do not tell them it's wrong within 30 days
- £400 if you submit a paper VAT Return, unless HMRC has told you you're exempt from submitting your return online

VAT Assessments

If you do not send your VAT Return and pay any VAT due on time, you will get a 'VAT notice of assessment of tax' from HM Revenue and Customs (HMRC), telling you how much VAT they think you owe.

To avoid VAT assessments, send your VAT Return and any payment due immediately.

If the assessed amount of VAT is too low, you must tell HMRC within 30 days. Do this by sending a correct VAT Return and VAT payment or contacting them. You may be charged a penalty if you do not.

If the assessment is too high, you cannot appeal it. You must send a correct VAT Return and VAT payment.

Contact HMRC if you cannot pay your tax bill and contact the VAT helpline if you cannot send the return.

Interest on underpaid or overpaid VAT

HM Revenue and Customs (HMRC) may charge you interest if you do not report and pay the right amount of VAT. If you pay too much VAT because HMRC make a mistake, you can claim interest.

HMRC may charge you Interest if you:
- report less VAT than you charge, or reclaim more than you pay
- pay an assessment that I IMRC later find was too low
- let HMRC know you owe them VAT because of a mistake on your VAT Return

The amount of interest you will be charged is 3%.

There is a different interest rate for tax that was underpaid before 21 November 2017. Use your VAT online account to check the amount you owe.

HMRC will also send you a notice telling you how much you owe and how it's worked out.

If you do not pay within 30 days, further interest is charged on the VAT due from the date of the notice. You'll be charged interest for as long as you do not pay, up to a maximum of 2 years.

You cannot deduct the interest HMRC charges you when working out your taxable profits.

On the other hand, you may be able to claim interest if HMRC makes a mistake and that mistake means:
- you pay too much VAT
- you reclaim too little VAT
- a payment to you from HMRC was delayed

How much interest can you claim?

You can claim 0.5% interest. This is normally paid for the whole period from when the VAT was overpaid or reclaimed until the date repayment is authorised. There is a different interest rate for tax that was overpaid before 29 September 2009.

If you caused a delay to any payments (for example by not claiming straight away) HMRC might leave this time out. You have to claim the interest separately from the repayment itself.

Write to HMRC with details of the repayment, explaining why you're owed interest. You must do this within 4 years of the repayment's authorisation date. Use the postal address on the VAT correspondence you have from HMRC.

Any interest you get from HMRC counts as taxable income.

Please note that HMRC will normally not repay interest if you've paid too much VAT because of a mistake you made.

Paying interest to your customers

You must pay any of the interest you get (as well as the VAT) to your customers if HMRC's mistake means they paid too much VAT.

Contact the person at HMRC who dealt with your claim if you need to find out how the interest was calculated. This can help you work out how much you need to repay each customer. You must give the money back to HMRC within 14 days if you cannot get in touch with a customer to repay them.

Interest rates

HMRC only charge or pay simple interest (*interest on the original amount, not interest on interest*).

Challenging an HMRC decision

You cannot appeal the decision to charge you interest but you can challenge the actual amount.

Notes

CANCELLING YOUR VAT REGISTRATION

You must cancel your registration if you are no longer eligible to be VAT registered. For example:

- you stop trading or making VAT taxable supplies
- you join a VAT group

You must cancel within 30 days if you stop being eligible or you may be charged a penalty.

You can ask HM Revenue and Customs (HMRC) to cancel your registration if your VAT taxable turnover falls below the deregistration threshold of £83,000.

How to cancel your VAT registration

You can cancel your VAT registration online or you can also fill in and send form VAT7 to deregister from VAT by post.

Once your VAT registration is cancelled, it usually takes 3 weeks for HMRC to confirm your deregistration and the official deregistration date. This is either the date when the reason for your cancellation took effect (for example, when you stopped trading), or the date you asked to deregister if it's voluntary.

HMRC will send confirmation to your VAT online account (or through the post if you do not apply online). From the date of deregistration you must stop charging VAT and keep your VAT records for 6 years.

HMRC will automatically re-register you if they realise you should not have cancelled. You'll have to account for any VAT you should have paid in the meantime.

Please note that you will have to submit a final VAT Return for the period up to and including the deregistration date. You can usually do this online using your VAT online account and you must account for any stock and other assets you have on this date if:

- you could reclaim VAT when you bought them
- the total VAT due on these assets is over £1,000

Do not wait until you've received all your invoices before submitting your final return. You'll still be able to reclaim VAT on anything you bought for your business while still registered once you get the invoices.

HMRC will send you a paper version to complete if your registration is cancelled because you are insolvent

Transferring a registration

You can transfer a VAT registration from one business to another, or if the status of your business changes.
For example, if:

- you take over a company and want to keep using its VAT number
- your business changes from a partnership to a sole trader

If you're taking over a company, the previous owner must cancel their VAT registration before you can apply to transfer the VAT number. If the status of your business changes, you must cancel your existing VAT registration and re-register.
You can apply to cancel or transfer a VAT registration:

- online - through your VAT online account
- by post - using form VAT68

Once you have done initiated the transfer, it usually takes 3 weeks for HMRC to confirm the transfer.

If you are selling your business:

- cancel your accountant's access to your VAT online account - for example if you authorised them to deal with your VAT
- cancel any direct debits on your VAT online account

You must also give your records to the buyer if you're passing on your VAT number.

If you are buying a business:

- contact HMRC within 21 days of the transfer application if you want to keep the seller's accountant
- replace any self-billing arrangements with new ones
- set up new direct debits on your VAT online account

You can cancel your VAT registration online or you can also fill in and send form VAT7 to deregister from VAT by post.

AFTERWORD AND CONCLUSION

I hope through this book that you have somewhat got something to help you understand and manage basic VAT compliance for your business or the company you work for. If you found this book helpful, why not leave me your comment or feedback at sterling@sterlinglibs.com I will really appreciate that.

Thank you for buying this book and using it.

I want to leave you with these words of encouragement to be be your best and stay that way:

Affirm, or say to yourself the following words to yourself whenever you can: *"I love myself, I love my work, and I am the best at what I do"*

Peace and Love
Sterling.

If you believe it, say it:
I like myself, I love my work and I
am the best at what I do. I have a
lavish income consistent with
integrity and mutual benefit.

OTHER BOOKS BY STERLING LIBS

No.	Book Title
1	<u>EMBOLDEN</u> – *Mastering the Art of Being Bold, Bold, Confident, and Courageous in Your Life, Every Day*
2	<u>THE TRAINEE ACCOUNTANT'S HANDBOOK</u> – *All You Need to Know About Having a Successful Accounting Career*
3	<u>PRACTICAL WORK EXPERIENCE IN ACCOUNTING</u> – *Step by Step Practical Guide Using Sage 50 Accounts*
4	<u>FINANCIAL ACCOUNTING</u> – *Practical Guide*
5	<u>AAT LEVEL 2: USING ACCOUNTING SOFTWARE</u> – *Practical guide with Screen shots and step by step process*
6	<u>HOW TO DO MONTH END ACCOUNTING PROCEDURES</u> – *Step by Step Practical Guide*
7	<u>THE ALL TIME SUCCESS PLANNER</u> – *The Master Plan for Achieving Your Goals in Record Time Without Stressing Yourself Out.*
8	<u>ADVANCED EXCEL FOR ACCOUNTANTS</u> – *Pivot Tables & VLOOKUP*
9	<u>HOW TO FILE ANNUAL ACCOUNTS & RETURN WITH HMRC AND COMPANIES' HOUSE</u>: *Detailed step by step practical experience guide*
10	<u>ACCOUNTING JOB QUESTIONS AND ANSWERS</u> - *Trainee Accountants Handbook*
11	<u>GETTING A NEW JOB</u> – *The Weekly Master Plan*

How to get these books:

1. Visit www.amazon.co.uk
2. Type in the name – Sterling Libs at the search bar on amazon.co.uk page and press enter or search.
3. Make your selection from the list that comes up and check out.
4. You can also get them from www.sterlinglibs.com

Printed in Great Britain
by Amazon

74736886R00050